CONSIDERATIONS REGARDING PROPOSALS TO GIVE LEGAL RECOGNITION TO UNIONS BETWEEN HOMOSEXUAL PERSONS

Congregation for
the Doctrine of the Faith

CONSIDERATIONS REGARDING PROPOSALS TO GIVE LEGAL RECOGNITION TO UNIONS BETWEEN HOMOSEXUAL PERSONS

BOOKS & MEDIA
BOSTON

ISBN 0-8198-1568-3

Vatican translation

No part of this booklet may be photocopied without written permission from the publisher.

Copyright © 2003, Daughters of St. Paul

Printed and published in the U.S.A. by Pauline Books & Media, 50 Saint Pauls Avenue, Boston MA 02130-3491.

www.pauline.org

Pauline Books & Media is the publishing house of the Daughters of St. Paul, an international congregation of women religious serving the Church with the communications media.

1 2 3 4 5 6 7 8   09 08 07 06 05 04 03

Contents

Introduction 9

I. The Nature of Marriage and Its Inalienable
Characteristics 11

II. Positions on the Problem of Homosexual
Unions 15

III. Arguments from Reason Against Legal
Recognition of Homosexual Unions 17

IV. Positions of Catholic Politicians with Regard to
Legislation in Favor of Homosexual Unions 23

Conclusion 25

Introduction

1. In recent years, various questions relating to homosexuality have been addressed with some frequency by Pope John Paul II and by the relevant Dicasteries of the Holy See.[1] Homosexuality is a troubling moral and social phenomenon, even in those countries where it does not present significant legal issues. It gives rise to greater concern in those countries that have granted or intend to grant legal recognition to homosexual unions, which may include the possibility of adopting children. The present considerations do not contain new doctrinal elements; they seek rather to reiterate the essential points on this question and provide

---

1. Cf. John Paul II, *Angelus Messages* of February 20, 1994, and of June 19, 1994; *Address to the Plenary Meeting of the Pontifical Council for the Family* (March 24, 1999); *Catechism of the Catholic Church,* nos. 2357–2359, 2396; Congregation for the Doctrine of the Faith, Declaration *Persona Humana* (December 29, 1975), 8; *Letter on the Pastoral Care of Homosexual Persons* (October 1, 1986); *Some Considerations Concerning the Response to Legislative Proposals on the Non-Discrimination of Homosexual Persons* (July 24, 1992); Pontifical Council for the Family, *Letter to the Presidents of the Bishops' Conferences of Europe on the Resolution of the European Parliament Regarding Homosexual Couples* (March 25, 1994); *Family, Marriage and "De Facto" Unions* (July 26, 2000), 23.

arguments drawn from reason which could be used by bishops in preparing more specific interventions, appropriate to the different situations throughout the world, aimed at protecting and promoting the dignity of marriage, the foundation of the family, and the stability of society, of which this institution is a constitutive element. The present considerations are also intended to give direction to Catholic politicians by indicating the approaches to proposed legislation in this area which would be consistent with Christian conscience.[2] Since this question relates to the natural moral law, the arguments that follow are addressed not only to those who believe in Christ, but to all persons committed to promoting and defending the common good of society.

---

2. Cf. Congregation for the Doctrine of the Faith, *Doctrinal Note on Some Questions Regarding the Participation of Catholics in Political Life* (November 24, 2002), 4.

I.
The Nature of Marriage and Its Inalienable Characteristics

2. The Church's teaching on marriage and on the complementarity of the sexes reiterates a truth that is evident to right reason and recognized as such by all the major cultures of the world. Marriage is not just any relationship between human beings. It was established by the Creator with its own nature, essential properties and purpose.[3] No ideology can erase from the human spirit the certainty that marriage exists solely between a man and a woman, who by mutual personal gift, proper and exclusive to themselves, tend toward the communion of their persons. In this way, they mutually perfect each other, in order to cooperate with God in the procreation and upbringing of new human lives.

3. The natural truth about marriage was confirmed by the revelation contained in the biblical accounts of creation, an expression also of the original human wisdom, in which

---

3. Cf. Second Vatican Council, Pastoral Constitution *Gaudium et Spes*, 48.

the voice of nature itself is heard. There are three fundamental elements of the Creator's plan for marriage, as narrated in the Book of Genesis.

In the first place, man, the image of God, was created "male and female" (Gen 1:27). Men and women are equal as persons and complementary as male and female. Sexuality is something that pertains to the physical-biological realm and has also been raised to a new level—the personal level—where nature and spirit are united.

Marriage is instituted by the Creator as a form of life in which a communion of persons is realized involving the use of the sexual faculty. "That is why a man leaves his father and mother and clings to his wife, and they become one flesh" (Gen 2:24).

Third, God has willed to give the union of man and woman a special participation in his work of creation. Thus, he blessed the man and the woman with the words "Be fruitful and multiply" (Gen 1:28). Therefore, in the Creator's plan, sexual complementarity and fruitfulness belong to the very nature of marriage.

Furthermore, the marital union of man and woman has been elevated by Christ to the dignity of a sacrament. The Church teaches that Christian marriage is an efficacious sign of the covenant between Christ and the Church (cf. Eph 5:32). This Christian meaning of marriage, far from diminishing the profoundly human value of the marital union between man and woman, confirms and strengthens it (cf. Mt 19:3–12; Mk 10:6–9).

4. There are absolutely no grounds for considering homosexual unions to be in any way similar or even remotely

analogous to God's plan for marriage and family. Marriage is holy, while homosexual acts go against the natural moral law. Homosexual acts "close the sexual act to the gift of life. They do not proceed from a genuine affective and sexual complementarity. Under no circumstances can they be approved."[4]

Sacred Scripture condemns homosexual acts "as a serious depravity... (cf. Rom 1:24–27; 1 Cor 6:10; 1 Tim 1:10). This judgment of Scripture does not of course permit us to conclude that all those who suffer from this anomaly are personally responsible for it, but it does attest to the fact that homosexual acts are intrinsically disordered."[5] This same moral judgment is found in many Christian writers of the first centuries[6] and is unanimously accepted by Catholic Tradition.

Nonetheless, according to the teaching of the Church, men and women with homosexual tendencies "must be accepted with respect, compassion and sensitivity. Every sign of unjust discrimination in their regard should be avoided."[7] They are called, like other Christians, to live the virtue of

---

4. *Catechism of the Catholic Church,* no. 2357.

5. Congregation for the Doctrine of the Faith, Declaration *Persona Humana* (December 29, 1975), 8.

6. Cf., for example, St. Polycarp, *Letter to the Philippians,* V, 3; St. Justin Martyr, *First Apology,* 27, 1-4; Athenagoras, *Supplication for the Christians,* 34.

7. *Catechism of the Catholic Church,* no. 2358; cf. Congregation for the Doctrine of the Faith, *Letter on the Pastoral Care of Homosexual Persons* (October 1, 1986), 10.

chastity.[8] The homosexual inclination is, however, "objectively disordered,"[9] and homosexual practices are "sins gravely contrary to chastity."[10]

---

8. Cf. *Catechism of the Catholic Church,* no. 2359; cf. Congregation for the Doctrine of the Faith, *Letter on the Pastoral Care of Homosexual Persons* (October 1, 1986), 12.

9. *Catechism of the Catholic Church,* no. 2358.

10. *Ibid.,* no. 2396.

II.
Positions on the Problem of Homosexual Unions

5. Faced with the fact of homosexual unions, civil authorities adopt different positions. At times they simply tolerate the phenomenon; at other times they advocate legal recognition of such unions, under the pretext of avoiding, with regard to certain rights, discrimination against persons who live with someone of the same sex. In other cases, they favor giving homosexual unions legal equivalence to marriage properly so-called, along with the legal possibility of adopting children.

Where the government's policy is *de facto* tolerance and there is no explicit legal recognition of homosexual unions, it is necessary to distinguish carefully the various aspects of the problem. Moral conscience requires that, in every occasion, Christians give witness to the whole moral truth, which is contradicted both by approval of homosexual acts and unjust discrimination against homosexual persons. Therefore, discreet and prudent actions can be effective; these might involve: unmasking the way in which such tolerance might be exploited or used in the service of ideology; stating clearly the immoral nature of these unions; reminding the government of the need to contain the phenomenon within certain limits so as to safeguard public morality and, above all, to avoid exposing young people to erroneous ideas about sexuality and marriage that would deprive them of their necessary defenses and contribute to the spread of the phenomenon. Those who would move from tolerance to the legitimization of specific rights for cohabiting homosexual persons need to be reminded that the approval or legalization of evil is something far different from the toleration of evil.

In those situations where homosexual unions have been legally recognized or have been given the legal status and rights belonging to marriage, clear and emphatic opposition is a duty. One must refrain from any kind of formal cooperation in the enactment or application of such gravely unjust laws and, as far as possible, from material cooperation on the level of their application. In this area, everyone can exercise the right to conscientious objection.

III.
Arguments from Reason Against Legal Recognition of Homosexual Unions

6. To understand why it is necessary to oppose legal recognition of homosexual unions, ethical considerations of different orders need to be taken into consideration.

From the order of right reason

The scope of the civil law is certainly more limited than that of the moral law,[11] but civil law cannot contradict right reason without losing its binding force on conscience.[12] Every humanly-created law is legitimate insofar as it is consistent with the natural moral law, recognized by right reason, and insofar as it respects the inalienable rights of every person.[13] Laws in favor of homosexual unions are contrary

---

11. Cf. John Paul II, Encyclical Letter *Evangelium Vitae* (March 25, 1995), 71.

12. Cf. *ibid.*, 72.

13. Cf. St. Thomas Aquinas, *Summa Theologiae*, I–II, q. 95, a. 2.

to right reason because they confer legal guarantees, analogous to those granted to marriage, to unions between persons of the same sex. Given the values at stake in this question, the State could not grant legal standing to such unions without failing in its duty to promote and defend marriage as an institution essential to the common good.

It might be asked how a law can be contrary to the common good if it does not impose any particular kind of behavior, but simply gives legal recognition to a *de facto* reality which does not seem to cause injustice to anyone. In this area, one needs first to reflect on the difference between homosexual behavior as a private phenomenon and the same behavior as a relationship in society, foreseen and approved by the law, to the point where it becomes one of the institutions in the legal structure. This second phenomenon is not only more serious, but also assumes a more wide-reaching and profound influence, and would result in changes to the entire organization of society, contrary to the common good. Civil laws are structuring principles of man's life in society, for good or for ill. They "play a very important and sometimes decisive role in influencing patterns of thought and behavior."[14] Lifestyles and the underlying presuppositions these express not only externally shape the life of society, but also tend to modify the younger generation's perception and evaluation of forms of behavior. Legal recognition of homosexual unions would obscure certain basic moral values and cause a devaluation of the institution of marriage.

---

14. John Paul II, Encyclical Letter *Evangelium Vitae* (March 25, 1995), 90.

From the biological and anthropological order

7. Homosexual unions are totally lacking in the biological and anthropological elements of marriage and family which would be the basis, on the level of reason, for granting them legal recognition. Such unions are not able to contribute in a proper way to the procreation and survival of the human race. The possibility of using recently discovered methods of artificial reproduction, beyond involving a grave lack of respect for human dignity,[15] does nothing to alter this inadequacy.

Homosexual unions are also totally lacking in the conjugal dimension, which represents the human and ordered form of sexuality. Sexual relations are human when and insofar as they express and promote the mutual assistance of the sexes in marriage and are open to the transmission of new life.

As experience has shown, the absence of sexual complementarity in these unions creates obstacles in the normal development of children who would be placed in the care of such persons. They would be deprived of the experience of either fatherhood or motherhood. Allowing children to be adopted by persons living in such unions would actually mean doing violence to these children, in the sense that their condition of dependency would be used to place them in an environment that is not conducive to their full human development. This is gravely immoral and in open contradiction to the principle, recognized also in the United Na-

---

15. Cf. Congregation for the Doctrine of the Faith, Instruction *Donum Vitae* (February 22, 1987), II, A, 1–3.

tions Convention on the Rights of the Child, that the best interests of the child, as the weaker and more vulnerable party, are to be the paramount consideration in every case.

From the social order

8. Society owes its continued survival to the family, founded on marriage. The inevitable consequence of legal recognition of homosexual unions would be the redefinition of marriage, which would become, in its legal status, an institution devoid of essential reference to factors linked to heterosexuality; for example, procreation and raising children. If, from the legal standpoint, marriage between a man and a woman were to be considered just one possible form of marriage, the concept of marriage would undergo a radical transformation, with grave detriment to the common good. By putting homosexual unions on a legal plane analogous to that of marriage and the family, the State acts arbitrarily and in contradiction with its duties.

The principles of respect and non-discrimination cannot be invoked to support legal recognition of homosexual unions. Differentiating between persons or refusing social recognition or benefits is unacceptable only when it is contrary to justice.[16] The denial of the social and legal status of marriage to forms of cohabitation that are not and cannot be marital is not opposed to justice; on the contrary, justice requires it.

---

16. Cf. St. Thomas Aquinas, *Summa Theologiae,* II–II, q. 63, a. 1, c.

Nor can the principle of the proper autonomy of the individual be reasonably invoked. It is one thing to maintain that individual citizens may freely engage in those activities that interest them and that this falls within the common civil right to freedom; it is something quite different to hold that activities which do not represent a significant or positive contribution to the development of the human person in society can receive specific and categorical legal recognition by the State. Not even in a remote analogous sense do homosexual unions fulfill the purpose for which marriage and family deserve specific categorical recognition. On the contrary, there are good reasons for holding that such unions are harmful to the proper development of human society, especially if their impact on society were to increase.

From the legal order

9. Because married couples ensure the succession of generations and are therefore eminently within the public interest, civil law grants them institutional recognition. Homosexual unions, on the other hand, do not need specific attention from the legal standpoint since they do not exercise this function for the common good.

Nor is the argument valid according to which legal recognition of homosexual unions is necessary to avoid situations in which cohabiting homosexual persons, simply because they live together, might be deprived of real recognition of their rights as persons and citizens. In reality, they can always make use of the provisions of law—like all citizens from the standpoint of their private autonomy—to protect their rights in matters of common interest. It would be gravely unjust to sacrifice the common good and just laws on the family in order to protect personal goods that can and must be guaranteed in ways that do not harm the body of society.[17]

---

17. It should not be forgotten that there is always "a danger that legislation which would make homosexuality a basis for entitlements could actually encourage a person with a homosexual orientation to declare his homosexuality or even to seek a partner in order to exploit the provisions of the law" (Congregation for the Doctrine of the Faith, *Some Considerations Concerning the Response to Legislative Proposals on the Non-Discrimination of Homosexual Persons* [July 24, 1992], 14).

IV.
Positions of Catholic Politicians with Regard to Legislation in Favor of Homosexual Unions

10. If it is true that all Catholics are obliged to oppose the legal recognition of homosexual unions, Catholic politicians are obliged to do so in a particular way, in keeping with their responsibility as politicians. Faced with legislative proposals in favor of homosexual unions, Catholic politicians are to take account of the following ethical indications.

When legislation in favor of the recognition of homosexual unions is proposed for the first time in a legislative assembly, the Catholic lawmaker has a moral duty to express his opposition clearly and publicly and to vote against it. To vote in favor of a law so harmful to the common good is gravely immoral.

When legislation in favor of the recognition of homosexual unions is already in force, the Catholic politician must oppose it in the ways that are possible for him and make his opposition known; it is his duty to witness to the truth. If it is not possible to repeal such a law completely, the Catholic politician, recalling the indications contained in the Encyclical Letter *Evangelium Vitae*, "could licitly support proposals aimed at limiting the harm done by such a law and at lessening its negative consequences at the level of general opinion and public morality," on condition that his "absolute personal opposition" to such laws was clear and well known and that the danger of scandal was avoided.[18] This does not mean that a more restrictive law in this area could be considered just or even acceptable; rather, it is a question of the legitimate and dutiful attempt to obtain at least the partial repeal of an unjust law when its total abrogation is not possible at the moment.

---

18. John Paul II, Encyclical Letter *Evangelium Vitae* (March 25, 1995), 73.

Conclusion

11. The Church teaches that respect for homosexual persons cannot lead in any way to approval of homosexual behavior or to legal recognition of homosexual unions. The common good requires that laws recognize, promote and protect marriage as the basis of the family, the primary unit of society. Legal recognition of homosexual unions or placing them on the same level as marriage would mean not only the approval of deviant behavior, with the consequence of making it a model in present-day society, but would also obscure basic values which belong to the common inheritance of humanity. The Church cannot fail to defend these values, for the good of men and women and for the good of society itself.

The Sovereign Pontiff John Paul II, in the audience of March 28, 2003, approved the present considerations, adopted in the Ordinary Session of this Congregation, and ordered their publication.

Rome, from the Offices of the Congregation for the Doctrine of the Faith, June 3, 2003, Memorial of Saint Charles Lwanga and his Companions, Martyrs.

Joseph Cardinal Ratzinger
Prefect

Angelo Amato, S.D.B.
Titular Archbishop of Sila
Secretary

Also available from

BOOKS & MEDIA

On the Pastoral Care of Homosexual Persons
and
Non-Discrimination Against Homosexual Persons

By the Congregation for the Doctrine of the Faith
#5138-8 $2.95

Declaration on Certain Questions ConcerningSexual Ethics

By the Congregation for the Doctrine of the Faith
#1846-1 $.50

Order today!

www.pauline.org
1-800-876-4463

BOOKS & MEDIA

The Daughters of St. Paul operate book and media centers at the following addresses. Visit, call or write the one nearest you today, or find us on the World Wide Web, www.pauline.org

CALIFORNIA
3908 Sepulveda Blvd, Culver City, CA 90230   310-397-8676
5945 Balboa Avenue, San Diego, CA 92111   858-565-9181
46 Geary Street, San Francisco, CA 94108   415-781-5180

FLORIDA
145 S.W. 107th Avenue, Miami, FL 33174   305-559-6715

HAWAII
1143 Bishop Street, Honolulu, HI 96813   808-521-2731
Neighbor Islands call: 800-259-8463

ILLINOIS
172 North Michigan Avenue, Chicago, IL 60601
312-346-4228

LOUISIANA
4403 Veterans Memorial Blvd, Metairie, LA 70006
504-887-7631

MASSACHUSETTS
885 Providence Hwy, Dedham, MA 02026   781-326-5385

MISSOURI
9804 Watson Road, St. Louis, MO 63126   314-965-3512

NEW JERSEY
561 U.S. Route 1, Wick Plaza, Edison, NJ 08817   732-572-1200

NEW YORK
150 East 52nd Street, New York, NY 10022   212-754-1110
78 Fort Place, Staten Island, NY 10301   718-447-5071

PENNSYLVANIA
9171-A Roosevelt Blvd, Philadelphia, PA 19114   215-676-9494

SOUTH CAROLINA
243 King Street, Charleston, SC 29401   843-577-0175

TENNESSEE
4811 Poplar Avenue, Memphis, TN 38117   901-761-2987

TEXAS
114 Main Plaza, San Antonio, TX 78205   210-224-8101

VIRGINIA
1025 King Street, Alexandria, VA 22314   703-549-3806

CANADA
3022 Dufferin Street, Toronto, Ontario, Canada M6B 3T5   416-781-9131
1155 Yonge Street, Toronto, Ontario, Canada M4T 1W2   416-934-3440

¡También somos su fuente para libros, videos y música en español!